They met the Lord Jesus

Daily Bible readings
introducing the Lord Jesus

Alec Taylor

 **BOOKS**

EP BOOKS
Faverdale North
Darlington
DL3 0PH, England

www.epbooks.org
sales@epbooks.org

EP BOOKS are distributed in the USA by:
JPL Fulfillment
3741 Linden Avenue Southeast,
Grand Rapids, MI 49548.

E-mail: sales@jplfulfillment.com
Tel: 877.683.6935

First published 2014

British Library Cataloguing in Publication Data available
ISBN: 978-1-78397-026-1

Contents

You will see from the above list that all readings are from the New Testament, which is the second part of the Bible.

Foreword

Many people claim to believe in Jesus, but do not really know what he is like. When Christians think about Jesus, the word 'GREATNESS' often comes to mind. Why is Jesus so great?

The Lord Jesus is the greatest Prophet ever to have walked this earth, but he is more than a Prophet. He is the holy Son of God who took a human body when he came into the world. Many consider his claim to be God's Son as blasphemy because this is the same as saying that he is God. The Bible, which is God's holy word, clearly affirms that Jesus is God and that he has always existed (John chapter 1, verses 1 to 18; Philippians chapter 2, verses 5 to 8).

The Bible teaches us that Jesus created all things (Colossians 1, verses 15 and 16). He created the vast galaxies and the world in which we live. He is the God who designed the smallest atom and the many beautiful things around us. He has infinite wisdom and power! The angels worship him (Hebrews chapter 1, verses 1 to 12). No prophet has ever been like him.

The Gospels do not give us any detailed physical description of the Lord Jesus and we do not know what he looked like. We cannot see him and we cannot know him in the same way as those who met him when he lived on earth. Most of those who met him, however, were astonished at his teaching, his wisdom and his power to heal the sick and to raise the dead.

Jesus is wonderful in all his ways, but not everyone welcomed him when he lived on earth; some even hated him. He said that he would suffer and die at the hands of wicked people and that he would rise from the dead. This happened just as he had prophesied. He appeared many times to his disciples over a period of forty days before he returned to heaven. We can know him as our Saviour, Lord and dearest Friend. This booklet has thirty-one undated Bible readings which introduce us to the Lord Jesus. I pray that all my readers will find it helpful.

Alec Taylor

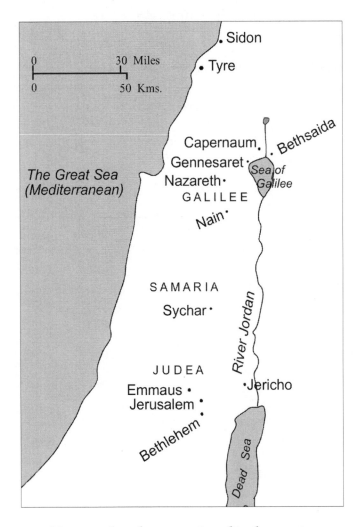

Map covering places mentioned in these notes

Key to notes

- All Scripture quotations are printed in italics.

- The number in brackets, e.g. (6) refers to the verse number in the passage that we are reading; (2:6) refers us to another chapter and verse in the book of the Bible we are reading. If we were reading from the Gospel of Matthew, this would be Matthew chapter 2, verse 6.

- Where verses from other books of the Bible are brought to our attention, the name of the book is also indicated in the brackets, e.g. (Psalm 19:1).

- Where I ask you to compare another verse of Scripture, I prefix the reference with cp. (e.g. cp. John 1:1). I prefer this to the more common abbreviation, cf., which relates to the obsolete word 'confer'.

Fearful shepherds

The Old Testament Scriptures contain many prophecies about the coming of a Saviour. He is known to the Jews as 'The Messiah', which means 'the anointed One'. In Israel kings and priests were anointed with oil when set apart for their important office. Another word for 'Messiah' is 'Christ'. The Lord Jesus is the promised Saviour. He is God's anointed One (cp. Psalm 2:2). The birth of the Messiah in Bethlehem was prophesied 600 years beforehand (Micah 5:2).

The coming of the Lord Jesus into the world is one of the most important events in history! God did not announce the birth of Christ to kings or religious leaders, but to humble shepherds who were guarding their flock at night. They experienced a sudden and unexpected visit from an angel, and were filled with fear at the dazzling sight. The angel reassured them, telling them not to fear because he was bringing them good news. *'For there is born to you this day in the city of David [Bethlehem] a Saviour, who is Christ the Lord'* (8-11). A multitude of angels joined him in praising God.

Once the angels had gone away, the shepherds hurried to Bethlehem where they found the holy infant in a manger (an animal feeding-trough) as the angel had said. The baby they saw that day was no ordinary infant. He is indeed the Saviour of the world! The shepherds returned to their flock, *glorifying and praising God for all the things that they had heard and seen* (20). **They would never forget that night when they saw angels and met the promised Saviour!** They had exciting news which they just had to share with others (17-18). The Christian message about the holy Son of God who came to earth to save sinners is wonderful and it is true. It is something to get excited about!

Note: The Holy Bible is divided into two sections: the Old Testament takes us from creation to just over four hundred years before the birth of Christ; the New Testament covers the coming of Christ into the world, his ministry and that of his apostles in the first century AD.

A popular preacher

Elizabeth, the mother of John the Baptist, was a relative of Mary, the mother of Jesus (Luke 1:36). They lived in different parts of the country and we haven't any record which shows that John met the Lord Jesus in his early years. John's preaching attracted huge crowds and many people wondered if he were the Messiah (the Christ).

When a delegation of priests and Levites from Jerusalem asked John: '*Who are you?*' he told them that he was not the Christ, nor Elijah, nor '*the Prophet*' (19-21, 24). The Jews were expecting Elijah to return to earth (Malachi 4:5). '*The Prophet*' is another term for the Messiah (Deuteronomy 18:15-18). This great preacher was a very humble man who pointed men away from himself to Christ (15, 23, 26-27). When an eastern king visited one of his provinces, a herald would go ahead of him to give the people time to prepare for the coming of the king. John was the herald who called on the people to prepare for the coming of the Christ among them.

John baptized those who repented of their sins, dipping them in the River Jordan. This was a symbol of the washing away of their sins. Bethabara, where John was baptizing (28), was about thirteen miles south of the Sea of Galilee, on the east bank of the Jordan. The sinless Lord Jesus asked for baptism (Matthew 3:13-14) to show his identification with sinful mankind by his coming to earth as a man.

When Jesus came to be baptized, John pointed him out as '*the Lamb of God who takes away the sin of the world*' (29). John also testified that Jesus *is the Son of God* who baptizes all who come to him with the Holy Spirit (33-34). This title of Jesus is very significant, showing his equality with God the Father. The Jewish leaders recognized his claim to be equal with God and they hated him for it (5:18). **The almighty Son of God died as a sacrificial Lamb to save sinners. How wonderful! That was John's message and it is ours too!** We are all sinners and we need to be saved. The only Saviour is the Lord Jesus Christ.

A respected religious teacher

Most of the religious leaders in Israel rejected the claims of the Lord Jesus (cp. John 5:18, 33-47), but one of them was different. Nicodemus, a respected Jewish teacher, had not closed his mind to the teaching of Jesus. He came to see the Lord Jesus one night to find out more about him. He recognized that Jesus was a Teacher from God and that his miracles were from God (1-2).

During his interview he discovered some very important truths. He learned that being religious does not guarantee a place in heaven. Like most Jews he would have believed that he was in the kingdom of God because of his Jewish birth. The Lord Jesus told him that he must be born again to enter the kingdom of God. We are all *born of the flesh* and have a sinful nature. *All have sinned* (6; cp. Romans 3:23). *Those who are in the flesh cannot please God* (Romans 8:8). We need a spiritual birth! Jesus said, '*You must be born again*' (7).

Nicodemus was puzzled and asked Jesus: '*How can these things be?*' (9). Jesus reminded him that God sent venomous serpents to punish the Israelites when they rebelled against him and his servant Moses. Many people were killed but others confessed their sin, begging Moses to pray for them. The Lord told him to make a serpent of brass and lift it up on a pole in the camp of Israel. All those who had been bitten were told to look at the serpent and those who did so were saved from death (Numbers 21). Jesus went on to tell him that he, Jesus, must be lifted up in order to save sinners (14). It would appear that Nicodemus later became a Christian (cp. 7:50-52; 19:39).

The Jews were expecting the Messiah to come to punish their enemies, but Jesus did not come to condemn the world. He was himself lifted up on a cross to save sinners (17). *For God so loved the world that he gave his only begotten Son, that whoever believes in him should not perish but have everlasting life* (16). **What marvellous love!** Whoever believes (trusts) in the Lord Jesus has everlasting life. They are born again and are admitted to God's kingdom.

An immoral Samaritan woman

The Lord Jesus *needed to go through Samaria* (4). This was the most direct route to Galilee from Judea but was not popular with Jews. Jesus had his own reason for taking this route. He was to bring a sinful woman and others in her city to faith in himself. Most Jews despised Samaritans who were a mixed race of Jew and Gentile. Like the Jews they too looked for the Messiah (25). When the enemies of Jesus wanted to insult him, they called him '*a Samaritan*' (John 8:48).

The Lord Jesus was resting by a well, when a Samaritan woman came to draw water. He asked her for a drink and this surprised her. Jews did not ask favours of Samaritans and no Jew would drink from a container used by Gentiles (6-7). Jesus then aroused her curiosity by speaking about '*the gift of God*' and '*living water*' (which she took to mean fresh spring water). How could he obtain such *living water* from such a deep well? Could this stranger be greater than Jacob (9-12)? Jesus told the woman that the water from the well could only satisfy for a time, '*but whoever drinks of the water that I shall give him will never thirst*' (14). She misunderstood Jesus and thought that he had some kind of water that once taken would quench her thirst for ever and do away with the need to draw and carry water (15).

He then told the woman to fetch her husband. When she denied having a husband, Jesus amazed her by revealing that he knew all about her immoral lifestyle (16-18). He touched a raw nerve and the embarrassed woman tried to change the subject, so she started to talk about religion in general. Was he a prophet? Where should we worship God? The astonished woman confessed that she knew that the coming Messiah would tell them all things (and Jesus had done this in her case). Jesus replied that he was that very Person (25-26). The woman forgot about water and hurried back to Sychar, saying to the men, '*Come, see a man who told me all things that I ever did. Could this be the Christ?*' (27-30). **She discovered the surpassing greatness of our Lord and Saviour on that memorable day. Have you?**

Angry hearers

The ministry of the Lord Jesus was acclaimed in the Jewish synagogues (14-15) but not in the synagogue of his own town of Nazareth. He stood up to read the Scriptures and was handed the scroll containing the prophecy of Isaiah. He told an attentive congregation that the Scripture he had read to them (Isaiah 61:2) was being fulfilled in their hearing (16-21). He was the Messiah promised in those verses.

The people marvelled at his *gracious words*, but they regarded him only as Joseph's son. They had heard of his miracles at Capernaum but they also wanted to see signs before they would be convinced of his claims. Jesus answered the proverb that was in their thoughts with another proverb: '*No prophet is accepted in his own country*' (22-24).

The Lord Jesus reminded his hearers that there were many widows in Israel in the days of Elijah, but God sent his prophet to a Gentile widow in Sidon. Moreover, the Syrian army commander Naaman was cleansed from his leprosy during Elisha's time but none of the many lepers in Israel were healed. *Then all those in the synagogue, when they heard these things, were filled with wrath* (28). They resented being told that God had bypassed the Jews in the past and had been merciful to Gentiles. Those who had earlier marvelled at *the gracious words* of Jesus were now filled with anger and attempted to kill him, but he was miraculously preserved (29-30).

Some believe that the Lord Jesus would be welcomed by everyone if he came back to earth to teach and to heal. That is not so! Blind prejudice still leads many to hate him and reject him. If they were able to see Jesus and witness his miracles, it would make little difference. They have closed their minds to the claims of Christ. **Please take care that you do not allow prejudice or anger to keep you from thinking carefully about the claims of the Lord Jesus.** If you reject him, you will never know forgiveness of sin, nor the peace and joy of God that he will bring to your life.

Four fishermen

Peter, Andrew, James and John were partners in a fishing business (7,10; cp. Mark 1:16-20). They had already become followers of the Lord Jesus and had recognized him as the Messiah (cp. John 1:35-51) but they were now called to leave their business interests to follow him.

A great crowd pressed about Jesus near to the spot where they were mending their nets and Peter readily allowed Jesus to teach from his boat. When Jesus finished teaching, he told Peter to take his boat into deeper water and to let down his net for a catch. Peter protested that they had toiled all night without success but said, *'Nevertheless at your word I will let down the net'* (5). Peter was to learn that to trust in Jesus and to obey him brings blessing. The net began to break under the strain of the great catch of fish, and James and John were summoned to help land the haul. **Jesus knew exactly where the experienced fishermen should fish because he knows all things and he is in control of all creation.**

An astonished and awestruck Peter worshipped Jesus, saying, *'Depart from me, for I am a sinful man, O Lord!'* (8-9). This was not a request for Jesus to go away but a recognition that he is God (*'Lord'* — cp. John 20:28; 2 Corinthians 4:5) and a confession of Peter's own sinfulness. Peter became a close friend and disciple of the Lord Jesus and he was to see his Master perform many more great miracles.

Jesus reassured Peter, saying to him, *'Do not be afraid. From now on you will catch men'* (10). Peter and his partners left their huge catch and their business interests to follow Jesus and to serve him. They had just seen the evidence that Jesus could supply all their needs. They were convinced that men and women needed to know the Lord Jesus as their Saviour and to be gathered into the wonderful kingdom of God. This is a far more important harvest than a harvest of fish! To be in God's kingdom and to know him as our heavenly Father brings great joy and peace to our lives.

A man with leprosy

These verses give an account of a memorable Sabbath in Capernaum. A man was delivered from demon-possession as he heard the Lord Jesus teaching in the synagogue. Jesus later healed Peter's mother-in-law (Peter is referred to by his other name of Simon in this chapter of Mark's Gospel). After sunset (when the Sabbath ended), many sick people were brought to Jesus and he healed them and cast out many demons. The Sabbath had been a very busy and exhausting day for the Lord Jesus but he rose *a long while before daylight ... and departed to a solitary place; and there he prayed* (35). The sinless Son of God spent much time with the Father in prayer (e.g. 6:46; 14:32; Luke 3:21; 6:12; 9:28; 11:1). Many in Capernaum were looking for Jesus, but he told the disciples that he had to preach in other towns (37-39).

A leper came to Jesus pleading to be healed, saying, '*If you are willing, you can make me clean*' (40). Leprosy was much feared in those times because it was incurable and people avoided lepers for fear of contracting the dreaded disease. Jesus was *moved with compassion* for the man and touched him (41). That touch would have meant so much to a man whom people feared to go near, but leprosy could not contaminate the holy Son of God. He was able to heal and cleanse the leprous man. As soon as Jesus said, '*I am willing; be cleansed*,' he was healed. Jesus warned the man not to tell anyone of this miracle apart from showing himself to the priest for ritual cleansing and confirmation of recovery so that he could return to normal life (44; cp. Leviticus 14:1-32). In his excitement he disobeyed the Lord and spread the news of his healing (45).

We all suffer from a plague worse than leprosy. That plague is sin, and we need to be forgiven and cleansed from our sin. **The Lord Jesus is willing to forgive us and to make us clean if we will come to him and ask him to save us.** He will never turn away those who come to him (John 6:37) and they know peace with God and joy as they follow him as their Lord.

A paralysed man

The Lord Jesus had been preaching throughout the province of Galilee before he returned to Capernaum (Mark 1:39). A great crowd thronged the house in which he was staying *and he preached the word to them* (1-2). Four men brought a paralysed man to him for healing but they could not get near to him because of the crowd. These resourceful men took the man up an outside stairway to the roof of the house. They opened up the roof and lowered him on his mattress. *When Jesus saw their faith*, he forgave the man's sins and healed him (5,11-12).

The scribes were the experts in religious law in New Testament times and were closely associated with the ultra-orthodox Pharisees. They rightly recognized that the Lord Jesus was claiming to be God when he told the man that his sins were forgiven. They thought that he was blaspheming because God alone can forgive sins. Jesus knew what they were thinking and he pointed out that he had authority to forgive sins (6-10). The Bible plainly teaches that the Lord Jesus is God. The title *'Son of Man'* is also a title of deity (10; cp. Matthew 26:64-65; Daniel 7:13-14). After the man was healed, they were all amazed, and they glorified God, saying, *'We never saw anything like this!'* (12).

The paralysed man had a great physical need but when his friends brought him to Jesus, an even greater need was met — his sins were forgiven! Jesus saw that their faith was not put off by the obstacle of the crowd thronging the house and he honoured that faith. It was a faith that persevered despite apparent setbacks. *Without faith it is impossible to please him* (Hebrews 11:6).

Faith is more than saying, 'I believe.' Christian faith is believing that what God says through the pages of the Bible is true. It also means that we trust in the Lord Jesus to save us from our sins and that we will love him and obey him. We cannot have peace with God without forgiveness of sin. **What kind of faith do you have?**

DAY 9   **Mark 2:13-17**

A tax collector

Levi is the same person as Matthew the Gospel writer (cp. Matthew 9:9). Tax collectors were hated and despised because they worked for the Romans who occupied their country. They also had a well-deserved reputation for being dishonest and corrupt. As long as they collected an agreed amount of tax for the Roman authorities, they could overcharge and keep the surplus for themselves. The tax payer had no right of appeal against the tax collector's levy. The scribes and Pharisees put them on the same level as the worst of sinners and wrote them off as far as salvation was concerned (16).

The Lord Jesus called Matthew, one of these social outcasts, to follow him and to be one of those most closely associated with him (14). His other name, Levi, means 'attached'. The tribe of Levi was attached to God in a special way, being set aside for the service of God. They provided the priests and teachers of God's law and others involved in the service and ritual of the temple. Matthew Levi had not attached himself to the Lord's work but to serve the heathen Romans. Can you imagine his amazement to hear the great Teacher, the holy Son of God, saying to him, '*Follow me*' (14)?

Matthew *arose and followed him* (14). He gave up a comfortable living to become attached to the Lord Jesus. He did not become a secret believer, but held a great feast to which he invited many other tax collectors where he introduced them to his Saviour. They too followed the Lord Jesus (15; cp. Luke 5:29).

No one is beyond the reach of God's mercy! Christianity is for sinners, but the churlish, self-righteous Pharisees did not recognize their own spiritual need. Jesus told them, '*I did not come to call the righteous, but sinners, to repentance*' (16-17). He does not call the righteous because there are no righteous people (Romans 3:10). We are all sinners and he calls us to repentance. When we answer his call, he receives us just as we are and freely forgives us. This is wonderful!

A helpless cripple

Jesus went to Jerusalem when there was a religious feast and came to the pool of Bethesda (1). A great crowd of sick people were sheltering under the five porches around the pool. They were hoping for a miracle when an angel stirred the waters (2-4). The Lord Jesus singled out a certain man who had been an invalid for thirty-eight years. He knew all about this man and he asked him, '*Do you want to be made well?*' (5-6). The man recognized his own helplessness (7). Jesus told him to take up his bed (a mat which could be rolled up like a sleeping bag) and to walk. The man was instantly healed (9)! The Lord Jesus brings hope where there is despair. Do you wonder why Christians love him and want to please him?

The Jews (probably Pharisees) were angry that Jesus healed the man at the pool on the Sabbath (9-12). They saw the man carrying his bed and this broke their man-made Sabbath laws, because he was carrying a 'burden'. These people lacked compassion and did not share the man's joy on account of his healing. He did not know that it was Jesus who had healed him until the Saviour sought him out in the temple (14).

There are some important principles to learn from this passage:

- Jesus knows all about you and your needs (6).
- Just as the man was unable to heal himself, we cannot save ourselves from our sin which enslaves us (8:34). We are dead in our sins until God works mightily in our lives through the Holy Spirit (Ephesians 2:1,5,8; Titus 3:5-6).
- We do not have to be enslaved by sin (8:34-36; Romans 6:14) but some love their sin and refuse to submit to the Lord Jesus (cp. 3:19). '*Do you want to be made well?*'

When the Jews discovered that it was Jesus who had healed the man, they were determined to kill him because he had done these things on the Sabbath (15-16). The opposition to Jesus became more intense after this incident, especially when he spoke of working in partnership with God the Father, as an equal (17-18).

Religious enemies

The scribes and Pharisees made Sabbath-keeping a great burden with all their petty rules and regulations. They were very quick to criticize the disciples for plucking ears of corn on the Sabbath in order to feed themselves (23-24). Jesus reminded them that King David, whom they respected, had done an unlawful thing by eating the showbread when hungry, but he was not condemned (25-26; cp. 1 Samuel 21:1-6).*

The Lord Jesus taught that human need must be met on the Sabbath just as it is on any other day. Mercy is far more important than outward religious observance and Jesus reminded them, '*The Son of Man is Lord even of the Sabbath*' (28). The Pharisees endured miserable, joyless Sabbaths but '*the Sabbath was made for man*' (27), not to be a burden but a blessing. The Sabbath is a gracious gift from God which should be the best day of every week for everyone.

There was a man in the synagogue with a withered hand and the Pharisees watched the Lord Jesus closely to see if he would heal him (3:1-2). He asked them: '*Is it lawful on the Sabbath to do good or to do evil, to save life or to kill?*' but they refused to answer him (4). He was angry and grieved by the hardness of their hearts and he then healed the man (5). The Pharisees had no compassion for the man and were annoyed to see him healed on the Sabbath. Although they were very rigid in their interpretation of the law, they plotted to murder the Lord Jesus on the Sabbath (6). **The disabled man saw the wrong kind of religion in the Pharisees. He then met the Lord Jesus who loved him and had pity on him. Jesus is wonderful in all his ways! Do you know him as your Saviour?**

* This incident occurred before David became king of Israel. He and the young men with him were very hungry, but the priest had no bread to give to them. David persuaded the priest to give them consecrated bread which only priests were allowed to eat. By taking the consecrated bread, David was violating God's law, but it was because he and his men were in great need of some food (1 Samuel 21:1-6).

A grief-stricken widow

We live in a world in which there is much misery, suffering and sorrow. The Bible tells us that sin came into the world through the sin of Adam, the first man, and that sin brings death. We will die because we are sinners by nature (Romans 5:12). The Christian message is that suffering and death will end when Jesus comes again (1 Corinthians 15:51-55; Revelation 21:3-5). We are reminded of the terrible effects of sin when death visits a family.

The Lord Jesus went to Nain, some twenty-five miles south-west of Capernaum, followed by a large crowd. As they approached the city, they were met by another large crowd. This crowd was following a weeping widow in a funeral procession. God is very concerned for widows. They are vulnerable and need our help (Exodus 22:22-23; Deuteronomy 14:28-29; 1 Timothy 5:3; James 1:27). This widow had lost her only son and *when the Lord saw her, he had compassion on her* (13). Jesus does not change! Our trials, troubles and tears do not go unnoticed. He is a wonderful Saviour and Friend who is full of compassion.

The Lord Jesus told the widow not to weep. He then touched the open coffin as the procession halted and said to the lifeless body, '*Young man, I say to you, Arise*' (14). Jesus did not need to pray to God for the raising of the dead because he is God (the title '*Lord*' in verse 13 also indicates his deity). He has power over sickness, over demons and over death. The young man sat up and the Lord Jesus presented him to his mother. Her grief was turned to joy. She discovered the greatness and kindness of our precious Saviour on that memorable day.

The crowds were awestruck and they glorified God, acknowledging Jesus as a great Prophet, saying, '*God has visited his people*' (15-16). **When God visits us, hopelessness and despair give way to hope and joy. When he comes to us, things are never the same again. Do you really know the Lord Jesus in your life and experience?**

A man possessed by demons

Demons are also known as evil or unclean spirits. A demon-possessed man met Jesus when he arrived in the country of the Gadarenes on the south-eastern shore of the Sea of Galilee. This poor wretch lived among the tombs and ran around wild, naked, shrieking and cutting himself with stones. He had superhuman strength through the power of the evil spirits which controlled him and chains could not hold him (26-29; cp. Mark 5:5). His encounter with Jesus teaches us two vital truths:

- That Jesus is God. The man fell down before the Lord Jesus, and the demon, speaking for the evil spirits within the man, said, '*What have I to do with you, Jesus, Son of the Most High God?*' (28). This title of Jesus shows that he is God. The Jews recognized that this title was one of deity (John 5:18; 10:36).

- That demons are subject to the Lord Jesus. They begged Jesus not to torment them (28). **The lovely presence of Jesus was a source of torment to these wicked spirits.** When confronted with Jesus, they were in the presence of One who is greater than their master, the devil. The demons left the man at the command of Jesus and entered a herd of pigs which ran over the cliffs to perish in the sea.

The terrified swineherds fled to the city to tell their story. The people of the city went to see what had happened and were afraid when they saw the man who had been previously possessed, *sitting at the feet of Jesus, clothed and in his right mind* (32-35). They did not welcome Jesus, however, nor did they bring their sick for healing, but *asked him to depart from them* (37). This is very sad. They had seen the evidence of the power of the Lord Jesus but they wanted nothing to do with him.

The man released from the demons was different, however. He begged Jesus that he might remain with him but Jesus told him to return to his own house to tell them what great things God had done for him. He needed no persuasion but *proclaimed throughout the whole city what great things Jesus had done for him* (38-39). **The Lord Jesus still does great things for those who trust in him.**

A woman with a discharge of blood

The Gadarene people did not want the Lord Jesus, but he was welcomed by a multitude when he returned to Galilee. Jairus, a ruler of the synagogue, came to Jesus begging him to come to his house to heal his dying daughter (40-42).

While Jesus was going to the house of Jairus, he was interrupted by a woman who was desperate to reach him for healing. This poor woman had suffered twelve years of misery through a discharge of blood. The continual loss of blood would have left her weak and she had desperately sought for relief. She had spent all that she had in search of a cure, without success (43).

The return of the Lord Jesus to Galilee gave her some hope, but she perceived that he was on a very urgent errand to go to the dying girl. She decided to touch the border of his garment in her desperate search for healing. Her condition would have rendered her unclean. Anyone touching someone in her condition would also be unclean (Leviticus 15:19-27). This probably explains why she did not want the Lord Jesus to know that she had touched his garment (47).

The discharge of blood instantly stopped when she touched his garment. She had received, in a moment, the healing that she had vainly sought for twelve years from many physicians. The Lord Jesus knew that someone had touched him in faith, for power had gone from him to heal the woman. He asked: *'Who touched me?'* and those around him denied doing so. The disciples were puzzled and Peter pointed out that many would have touched him in the thronging crowd. The woman was very much afraid and she fell down before Jesus and told him why she had touched him and how she had been instantly healed.

She discovered that day that the Lord Jesus is not only immensely powerful, but also wonderfully understanding and kind. He gently reassured her and commended her for her faith. He told her to *go in peace* (48). She believed that Jesus was able to heal her and he did.

An anxious father

The delay caused by the woman's healing and the Lord's conversation with her must have sorely tried the faith of Jairus. While Jesus was still speaking to the woman, Jairus heard the news that he had dreaded. His daughter had died. Death is a terrible enemy which visits every home. It has no respect of persons, whether they are rich or poor. There have been great advances in medical science and in the treatment of disease, but death still conquers, bringing great sorrow. The messenger thought that it was pointless troubling the Lord Jesus any further. In his grief and sorrow Jairus heard the wonderful words of Jesus, '*Do not be afraid; only believe, and she will be made well*' (50). The Lord Jesus wanted Jairus to trust him, even in this darkest hour.

In Bible times professional mourners were called in when someone died. They were experts in the art of weeping and wailing, moaning and groaning (cp. Jeremiah 9:17-18). Their performance turned to scornful laughter when Jesus told them that the girl was not dead but sleeping. He put out all the mourners, only permitting the girl's parents and Peter, James and John to go into the room where the lifeless child was lying.

When a Jew touched a dead body, he was rendered ritually unclean (Numbers 19:11). The holy Son of God is not affected by ritual uncleanness. He took the hand of the girl and said, '*Little girl, arise*' (54). She was instantly raised from the dead and Jesus commanded that she be given something to eat. Her parents were astonished when they saw this great miracle (56). They met Jesus that memorable day, and found that he is not only full of compassion, but that he is also the mighty Lord over death.

When the Lord Jesus comes again, all the dead will hear his voice and be raised either to be condemned for ever, or to have everlasting life in heaven (John 5:28-29). **If you want to have and to enjoy everlasting life, come to Jesus and pray, asking him to forgive your sin. It will be too late after you die, or when Jesus comes again.**

A boy who shared his lunch

The feeding of the five thousand is the only miracle of Jesus which is recorded in all four Gospels. This miracle occurred between six months and a year after the healing of the man at the pool (5:1-16). This period, on which John is silent, is covered in Luke 6:1 - 9:10 and Mark 3:1 - 6:30. During the same period the Lord Jesus taught 'The Sermon on the Mount' (Matthew 5 - 7).

Jesus had gone to the mountain to be alone with his disciples, but the crowds followed him, attracted by the miracles which he had performed (2; cp. Mark 6:30-33) and they became hungry. The Lord asked Philip where they could buy bread. *But this he said to test him, for he himself knew what he would do* (5-6). Though Philip had already seen great miracles, such as the turning of water into wine, he did not have miracles in his thinking. He could not see how such a huge crowd could be fed; two hundred denarii worth of bread would have hardly fed them. Two hundred denarii represent two hundred days' wages (7).

Andrew introduced to Jesus a lad who had five barley loaves and two fish (9). The Lord Jesus told his disciples to make the people sit down. He then took the loaves and gave thanks and distributed the bread to the disciples with the fish. Here was a great miracle! Every person in the crowd was fed with plenty to spare (10-13). The crowd responded to this miracle by acknowledging that Jesus was *'the Prophet'* (or 'the Messiah'; cp. Deuteronomy 18:15-18). **The boy who shared his lunch was privileged to witness the miraculous power of the Lord Jesus.**

The crowd wanted to make Jesus their King but he slipped away from them to be alone on a mountain (15). They did not realize that his kingdom is not political or earthly. They wanted a miracle-worker to meet their needs (26), but they were not willing to follow him in obedience to his word and in self-denial. **Have you asked Jesus to be your Lord and Saviour, or is something holding you back?**

DAY 17   **Matthew 14:22-33**

Twelve frightened disciples

Jesus sent the disciples ahead of him to cross the Sea of Galilee to Gennesaret (22,34). He spent time alone in prayer before walking on a wind-tossed sea to the disciples' boat. They were terrified when they saw him, believing that they had seen a ghost. Jesus calmed them with the words, '*Be of good cheer! It is I; do not be afraid*' (25-27). The Greek for '*It is I*' ('*ego eimi*') is literally 'I am', which is the covenant name of God (Exodus 3:14). The Jews recognized this when Jesus used the expression on another occasion, and they attempted to stone him for blasphemy (John 8:58-59). Jesus is God! His enemies understood his claims but they rejected him (cp. John 5:18).

Peter's entry into the stormy sea was no foolhardy venture of faith. He was beckoned by Jesus to walk on the water and all was well until he saw the storm around him. Perhaps the reason his faith failed him was that he took his eyes off the Lord. Jesus heard his cry for help, took him by the hand, and as they got into the boat, the storm abated. The amazed disciples knew that their Master was no ordinary man. He is the Son of God who is worthy of our worship (28-33).

The disciples had no need to fear when their Lord was with them, but, oh, the dullness and hardness of their hearts! They were greatly amazed at the demonstration of the Lord's power over the sea, but hadn't they already seen his divine power in multiplying the loaves and fish? (cp. Mark 6:51-52). **Why should they fear when they had such a Saviour, such a Friend? Why should we fear if we are true Christians?** '*Be of good cheer! It is I; do not be afraid.*'

When Jesus and the disciples landed on the shore of Gennesaret they were soon surrounded by huge crowds seeking healing. Everyone who touched the hem of Jesus' garment was healed (36). They too recognized that Jesus was no ordinary man. Have you trusted in him? Have you experienced his power in your life, saving you from your sin and transforming you?

A distraught mother

Jesus left Galilee to go to the region of Tyre and Sidon (21). A woman of Canaan came to the Saviour pleading that he cast a demon out of her daughter (22). She was a Gentile (non-Jew) but she had obviously heard of the Lord Jesus. She was in much distress and anguish because her beloved daughter was severely demon-possessed. At first, the Lord Jesus did not answer the woman, and his disciples, tired of her pleading, urged him to send her away (23).

The woman worshipped Jesus and pleaded, '*Lord, help me!*' (25). His attitude to the woman may have appeared harsh and indifferent, but he was testing her faith — and what great faith she had! She was not put off by the Lord's silence nor the unfriendly attitude of the disciples. She persisted in her pleading, even though Jesus said that the '*children's bread*' was not for '*the little dogs*' (in other words, he had come to minister to the Jews). The woman pointed out that '*the little dogs eat the crumbs which fall from their masters' table.*' She asked for some crumbs and her faith pleased the Lord Jesus. He said to her, '*O woman, great is your faith*', and he delivered her daughter from the demon that very hour (28).

Faith is important because without faith we cannot please God (Hebrews 11:6). Those who have great faith focus their trust in God, who is great. Great faith also perseveres in the face of discouragement. **Without faith you cannot be a Christian!** We must believe (trust) in the Lord Jesus, who died on the cross and rose from the grave to save us from our sins. *For God so loved the world that he gave his only begotten Son, that whoever believes in him should not perish but have everlasting life* (John 3:16).

The Canaanite woman's prayer was quite simple: '*Lord, help me!*' (25). No one else could help her in her need. Only Jesus was great enough to bring healing and peace to her poor daughter. She persisted in seeking the Lord's help and she was not disappointed.

Eyewitnesses of his majesty

The Lord Jesus took three of his disciples, Peter, James and John, to a high mountain where they were privileged to see his glory and splendour. His face was radiant, shining brighter than the sun. They saw the Lord Jesus as they had never seen him before!

The Lord Jesus was speaking with Moses, who had been dead almost 1500 years, and with Elijah who had been taken up to heaven 900 years earlier. They had come down from heaven to speak with the Lord Jesus about his death (Luke 9:31). Moses represents the Law, and Elijah the Prophets. The Lord Jesus has fulfilled the Law and the Prophets through his life and death (Luke 24:25-27, 44-46).

Peter suggested to the Lord Jesus that they made three tabernacles (tents), one each for Jesus, Moses and Elijah. While he was speaking, a bright cloud overshadowed them. The voice of God was heard coming from the cloud, *'This is my beloved Son, in whom I am well pleased. Hear him!'* (5). On hearing this, the disciples were filled with fear and fell on their faces. The Lord Jesus then came and touched them, telling them to get up and not be afraid. He told them not to tell anyone about the things that they had seen until he had risen from the dead (9).

The three men had seen Jesus perform many miracles and they had been taught by the greatest Prophet and Teacher. They had never before seen him in such brilliance and majesty, however. The transfiguration of Jesus was to have a lasting impression upon them. John wrote: *'We beheld his glory, the glory as of the only begotten of the Father, full of grace and truth'* (John 1:14). Peter records, *'We ... were eyewitnesses of his majesty'* (2 Peter 1:16-17). **They saw his dazzling splendour. They were convinced that he is no ordinary man but the holy One sent from heaven.**

A woman caught in the act

The woman was terrified. She had been caught in the act of adultery and she must have wondered how she would be punished for her sin. The scribes and Pharisees were quite prepared to have the full rigour of the law imposed upon her and have her stoned to death. The Lord Jesus was teaching in the temple when they brought this woman to him.

They reminded Jesus that according to the law of Moses she should be stoned to death (2-5). We may wonder why they did not also bring the man, because the law required that both guilty parties be put to death (Leviticus 20:10; Deuteronomy 22:22). They thought that they had put Jesus in an impossible situation (6). If he answered that she should be put to death, he could have been accused of undermining Roman civil authority for only the Romans could enforce the death penalty. If he said that she should be spared they would have accused him of denying the law of Moses.

Jesus pretended not to hear them and stooped down to write on the ground (we have no idea what he was writing; any speculation is futile). His agitated enemies pressed him for an answer and, rising up, he said, *'He who is without sin among you, let him throw a stone at her first'* (7; the law required the accuser to cast the first stone, Deuteronomy 17:7). Jesus returned to his writing, and his enemies, smitten in conscience, crept away one by one (8-9).

Seeing that there was no one left to accuse the woman, Jesus said to her, *'Neither do I condemn you; go and sin no more'* (11). Some people use this verse to justify their sinful ways, conveniently forgetting that though Jesus freely forgives repentant sinners, they must also cease their sinful lifestyle.

The woman found that the Lord Jesus is merciful and kind and that he freely forgave her. No one is too bad to be saved. If we sincerely repent of our sin and trust in him, he will accept us and forgive us.

A blind man

Jesus and his disciples saw a blind beggar and the disciples speculated on the cause of his blindness (1-2). We are all sinful by nature, but they wondered if there were some sin for which the man was being punished. The Lord Jesus said that this was not the reason for the man's condition. He had compassion on him and anointed his eyes with clay. He then sent him to wash his eyes at the pool of Siloam. The man was healed and his neighbours and others who had known him were amazed to see him with his sight and asked him how this had happened (8-10). He told them that '*a man called Jesus*' had healed him.

The Pharisees saw the man after he was healed and he told them his story, but they did not rejoice at the healing. They were furious that Jesus had again been healing on the Sabbath day, though some of them questioned how Jesus could do such miracles if he were a sinner (13-16). They then asked the man his opinion of Jesus and he replied that Jesus was '*a prophet*' (17).

They then questioned his parents who confirmed that their son had been born blind, but were fearful of saying any more. They knew that if they confessed that Jesus was the Christ (the Messiah), they would be put out of the synagogue. Religious exclusion would make them social outcasts (17-22). The man was not intimidated by the enemies of Jesus, however. When they again asked him how he had been healed, he responded to their doubts about Jesus, saying, '*One thing I know: that though I was blind, now I see*' (25).

The man bravely acknowledged that Jesus was from God and they excommunicated him (30-34). Jesus knew all about the rejection and suffering of the man he had healed. He sought, found and encouraged him (34-35). Jesus asked him: '*Do you believe in the Son of God?*' (35-38) and then revealed that he himself was the Son of God (35). **The man received spiritual sight as he worshipped not just a man (11), nor a prophet (17), but the Son of God (35-38). As we follow Christ, we discover just how great he really is.**

A disappointed young man

A young man came to Jesus with an important question. He asked him: *'What good thing shall I do that I may have eternal life?'* (16). He was rich and esteemed in religious circles; he was a ruler (probably an official in charge of the local synagogue, Luke 18:18). He called Jesus 'good', which was a confession that Jesus is God (16-17).

This young man was wealthy and religious, but he recognized that eternal life cannot be obtained with money or by religious observance (16). The Lord Jesus told him, *'If you want to enter life, keep the commandments'* (17). He asked Jesus: *'Which ones?'* and Jesus repeated several of the Ten Commandments. The young man said to him, *'All these things I have kept from my youth. What do I still lack?'* (18-20). He may have sincerely felt that he had kept the Ten Commandments but he was ignorant of the state of his own heart. We sin and break God's commandments from a very early age!

The Lord Jesus told him his problem. He must sell all that he had, give to the poor and follow him. He would then have treasure in heaven (21). This was too much for the young man. He wanted to have eternal life, but he also wanted to hold on to his possessions. He made his wealth an idol which he put before God; this proved that he was guilty of breaking the first commandment. Had he given away his wealth, it would have been an evidence of his repentance, his trust in Christ and his devotion to him.

His riches meant more to him than having eternal life. *He went away sorrowful* (22) because he was not willing to face up to the cost of following the Lord Jesus. This involves getting rid of anything that has become a 'god' in our lives. Many have turned away from the Christian faith disillusioned because they find the cost of following Jesus too great. There is a price to pay for treasure in heaven, but what blessing is enjoyed by all who truly follow Christ! **There is a greater price to pay for refusing to follow Christ — an eternity of separation from God.**

A dishonest rich man

The Lord Jesus went through Jericho on his way to Jerusalem (1). Jericho was famous for its fragrant balm derived from the balsam tree and was an important trading centre which yielded high taxes for the Roman government.

A man named Zacchaeus was the chief tax collector for that region. His name means 'righteous' or 'pure', but he appears to have been a scoundrel, who had become rich through fraud (2,7-8). He was curious to see Jesus, perhaps because he had heard that Jesus received tax collectors (who were hated and despised by most people; 15:1-2). Zacchaeus was small and unable to see Jesus because of the crowd. He was so determined, however, that he ran ahead of the crowd and climbed up into a sycamore tree (3-4; this fruit-bearing evergreen tree is not to be confused with the British or American sycamore trees; cp. Amos 7:14).

Zacchaeus managed to see Jesus from the tree and you can imagine his surprise when Jesus called him by name. He told the tax collector to be quick and to come down from the tree because he wished to stay at his house. The crowd murmured against Jesus for going into the house of such a sinner whom they considered to be far from God. He was an outcast, and not a Jew, as far as they were concerned. Zacchaeus was transformed as he came to faith in Christ and promised to give away half of his possessions to the poor and to restore fourfold to those he had defrauded (8). Jesus said that salvation had come to his house and that Zacchaeus was '*a son of Abraham*' (a true Jew), '*for the Son of Man has come to seek and to save that which was lost*' (9-10).

When Zacchaeus met the Lord Jesus, he found the Saviour knew all about him. Jesus knew about his wickedness, but was still willing to receive him and to forgive his sins. **He knows about you too! If you come to him, repenting of your sins, he will forgive you and save you. He will gladly receive you. No one is too sinful for Jesus to save.**

A man with a question

The scribes and the Pharisees were generally hostile to the Lord Jesus. They were not sincere in their questions put to him in this chapter (13). The scribes were also known as 'lawyers' — see Matthew 22:35. They were experts in interpreting and applying the Old Testament laws to everyday religion. Many of them were convinced that Jesus had come to destroy the law, but that was not so. He had stated quite plainly: '*Do not think that I came to destroy the Law or the Prophets. I did not come to destroy but to fulfil*' (Matthew 5:17). It is true that Jesus refused to endorse the petty rules that they had superimposed upon God's word. He was not destroying the law, only rejecting man-made traditions.

The scribes loved religious debates and one of their number asked Jesus a question which was typical of those which they debated: '*Which is the first commandment of all?*' (28). Jesus replied by quoting from the Old Testament (Deuteronomy 6:4-5 and Leviticus 19:18). Those verses repeated in verses 29 and 30 were used to open the worship in the Jewish synagogues and this custom is still observed. The verses are called 'The Shema' (taken from the first word *hear* which is '*shema*' in Hebrew).

The Lord Jesus answered the scribe: '*You shall love the Lord your God with all your heart, with all your soul, with all your mind, and with all your strength*' (30). Jesus also told the scribe that the second commandment is to love our neighbour as we love ourselves (31). The scribe acknowledged that Jesus had answered him well. He agreed that to obey the two great commandments is more important than observing religious ritual (32-33). This was a surprising answer for a scribe! Jesus encouraged him, saying, '*You are not far from the kingdom of God*' (34). The scribe recognized the supreme importance of love for God. He was religious, but he was not inside the kingdom of God. **If you are satisfied with being '*not far from the kingdom of God*', you will be shut out of it for ever. If you are '*not far from the kingdom of God*,' do not rest until you are in the kingdom.**

The Roman governor

The Lord Jesus had been arrested by his enemies who were determined that he be put to death. They needed the sanction of the Roman governor, however. Imagine the scene when the chief priests and elders arrived with their prisoner at the governor's residence. They hurled one accusation after another at the Lord Jesus but he did not speak, except for confirming that he was the King of the Jews. The governor, Pilate, *marvelled greatly* that Jesus did not seek to defend himself against his accusers (11-14).

Pilate knew that Jesus was innocent and had been delivered to him because of the envy of the leaders of the Jews (18,24). There was a custom at Passover for the governor to set a prisoner free at the request of the people. Pilate saw this as an opportunity to release the innocent Jesus and gave them a stark choice. He would release a murderer, Barabbas, or Jesus (15-17; cp. Luke 23:19). Surely they would ask for the release of Jesus rather than Barabbas? The plan failed, however. The wicked chief priests and elders were determined that Jesus should die. They persuaded the crowd to press for the release of the notorious criminal, and to call for the crucifixion of Jesus (20-23).

Pilate's wife had suffered a nightmare about Jesus and sent a message to her husband. She pleaded: '*Have nothing to do with this just man*' (19). How did Pilate respond to her pleading? *He took water and washed his hands* (24) but he could not escape his responsibility by protesting his innocence.

We, too, are faced with the challenge of Christ. We may not hate him like the crowd and their leaders, but we may reject him, because, like Pilate, we do not want to be involved with him. We cannot be neutral in our attitude to Christ. We either own him as our Saviour and Lord or we reject him! **It is no use pretending that we have no sin and have no need of a Saviour. We cannot wash our hands of Jesus and escape God's judgement.** If we reject Christ, we will be lost eternally. How is it with you?

A dying criminal

The Lord Jesus was executed with two murderers. He prayed for those who had condemned him and crucified him, '*Father, forgive them, for they do not know what they do*' (32-34). The people and their leaders taunted Jesus, saying, '*He saved others; let him save himself if he is the Christ, the chosen of God*' (35). Those words had a far deeper significance than his enemies realized. He could have saved himself and come down from the cross, but he would not! He was *obedient to the point of death* (Philippians 2:8) to fulfil God the Father's plan to save sinners (Acts 2:23).

One of the murderers crucified with Jesus blasphemed him and challenged him to save himself, and them also, if he were truly the Christ (39). He displayed no sorrow for his wickedness, nor did he trust in the Lord to save him. The other criminal rebuked him, becoming aware of the fear of God, of his own guilt, and of the power of Jesus to save him (40-42). Though the Lord Jesus was dying, this man trusted in him. He may never have witnessed any of the miracles of Jesus, but as he hung on a cross alongside the Lord Jesus, he displayed great faith.

The man was wonderfully saved even as he hung dying on a cross! He may never have prayed in his life, but his simple prayer was all that was needed. '*Lord, remember me when you come into your kingdom.*' He confessed Jesus as Lord and he really believed that Jesus had a kingdom over which he would be seen to reign.

Jesus assured the repentant criminal that he would be with him in heaven that very day (43; '*paradise*' = 'heaven'; cp. 2 Corinthians 12:2-4). No one is beyond the reach of the grace and mercy of God, even when they are dying. This is good news! **Two criminals met the Lord Jesus in the most distressing and fearful circumstances. One was saved and went to heaven, but the other was lost for ever.**

Faithful women

There was an earthquake when Jesus rose from the dead. An angel of the Lord came and rolled back the stone which had sealed the tomb. Some faithful women wanted to anoint the body of Jesus but had waited until the Sabbath ended (the Jewish Sabbath runs from sunset on Friday to sunset on Saturday). They went to the tomb early on Sunday morning and were the first to discover that it was empty. They saw the angel, who told them not to fear, and that Jesus had risen from the grave. He called on them to see the empty tomb and said to them, '*Go quickly and tell his disciples that he is risen from the dead*' (1-7).

The women were filled with awe and great joy as they left the tomb. They were then met by the risen Saviour who said to them, '*Rejoice!*' **In worshipping Jesus, the women recognized him to be God (9; cp. 4:10).** He repeated the message of the angel, '*Do not be afraid. Go and tell*' (10). The resurrection of Jesus is good news. Christ's resurrection declares him to be *the Son of God with power* (Romans 1:4). Death could not hold him (Acts 2:24). He triumphed over the grave and his resurrection is a guarantee that all who belong to him will be raised at his coming to have new bodies which will be immune to weakness, pain, ageing and suffering (John 14:19; 1 Corinthians 15:20-28; Philippians 3:20-21; 1 John 3:1-3). This wonderful news is a great comfort to all Christians.

The chief priests and the Pharisees knew that the terrified guards were not lying when they reported the events of the morning, but they bribed them to say that the disciples had stolen the body of Jesus (11-15). Their unbelief was wilful and deliberate. They had seen many miracles during the ministry of the Lord Jesus and they now knew that his prophecy of his resurrection from the dead was true (27:62-66). **They had closed their minds to the Christian message and many people do the same today.** Jesus once said, '*If they do not hear Moses and the prophets, neither will they be persuaded though one rise from the dead*' (Luke 16:31).

Two disconsolate followers of Jesus

Two followers of Jesus were travelling the seven miles from Jerusalem to Emmaus on the same day that he rose from the dead. While they were discussing all that had recently happened, the Lord Jesus joined them but they were prevented from recognizing him. He asked them what they were talking about and why they were so sad. One of them, Cleopas, was puzzled that he had been in Jerusalem and did not know what things had happened. Jesus asked them: *'What things?'* They told him how Jesus of Nazareth, who was a great Prophet, had been condemned by the chief priests and rulers and had been crucified. They had not been convinced by reports that Jesus had risen from the dead (13-24). Their hope that he would have redeemed Israel was crushed.

Jesus said to them, *'O foolish ones, and slow of heart to believe in all that the prophets have spoken!'* He then proved from the Scriptures that the Messiah had to suffer and to die before entering his glory (25-27). As they approached Emmaus, they persuaded the stranger to stay with them. **He prayed before they ate, and as he passed bread to them, their eyes were opened to recognize him.** He then vanished from their sight and they remembered how their hearts had burned within them when he opened the Scriptures to them (28-32).

The excited pair returned to Jerusalem that very hour to share their good news with the disciples of Jesus. On their arrival they were greeted with the news that the Lord had risen, and had appeared to Simon Peter. They then told their wonderful story to the disciples (31-35). As they were speaking, Jesus himself stood among them and said, *'Peace to you'* (36). They thought that they had seen a ghost and were terrified. He reassured them, inviting them to feel him and saying, *'A spirit does not have flesh and bones as you see I have.'* He then ate with them and *opened their understanding, that they might comprehend the Scriptures* (37-45). **Jesus is greater than any prophet! He is the holy Son of God who came into the world to save sinners through his death on the cross. The wonderful news is that he is alive today!**

A pessimistic doubter

Thomas was a pessimist (11:16) and he was not with the other disciples when the Lord Jesus first appeared to them. They told him, '*We have seen the Lord.*' Thomas would have dearly loved to believe that Jesus had risen from the dead, but he wanted to be sure that the others had not imagined that the Master had appeared to them. He said to the other disciples, '*Unless I see in his hands the print of the nails, and put my finger into the print of the nails, and put my hand into his side, I will not believe*' (25). He wanted to see and feel the risen Saviour before he would believe. **We must be careful to distinguish between the doubts of those who rebel against God, and the doubts suffered by the Christian.** There are those who oppose God with mocking and scoffing. Such rebels come under his judgement (2 Peter 3:3-7).

The Lord Jesus knew all about Thomas, his doubts and struggles. He knew what he had said to his fellow disciples. He appeared to the disciples a week later and on this occasion Thomas was with them. Jesus did not rebuke Thomas for his unbelief but was gentle with the struggling doubter. He said to him, '*Reach your finger here, and look at my hands; and reach your hand here, and put it into my side*' (27). He encouraged Thomas, saying to him, '*Do not be unbelieving but believing.*'

Thomas was now convinced that Jesus had indeed risen from the dead and he exclaimed, '*My Lord and my God!*' (28). **Thomas met with the risen Lord Jesus and his doubts fled away. He knew that Jesus is no ordinary man. He is God!** Jesus said to him, '*Thomas, because you have seen me, you believe. Blessed are those who have not seen and yet have believed*' (29). We have not yet seen the Lord Jesus, so *we walk by faith, not by sight* (2 Corinthians 5:7), but he blesses us when we trust in him.

A man who hated Christians

Saul of Tarsus was a devout Jew, who was relentless in his mission to destroy the church (1-2; cp. 8:1-3), but the more he persecuted Christians, the greater the growth of the church. Followers of Christ were now to be found in Damascus, about one hundred and fifty miles to the north of Jerusalem. Saul was determined that they should be arrested and brought back to Jerusalem for imprisonment. As he approached Damascus at midday, he was suddenly blinded by a dazzling light from heaven (3; 22:6). The risen Lord Jesus spoke to him, saying, '*Saul, Saul, why are you persecuting me?*' (4). Those who persecute believers persecute Christ.

God blinded Saul and humbled him so that he was now trembling with fear and astonishment. He asked two questions:

- '*Who are you, Lord?*' (5). The risen Saviour answered him: '*I am Jesus, whom you are persecuting. It is hard for you to kick against the goads.*' Saul had been kicking against a guilty conscience! He was to discover that Jesus is the holy Son of God (20), spoken of in the Old Testament Scriptures, who died to save sinners. We cannot be saved unless we know who Jesus is, and why he came into the world.

- '*Lord, what do you want me to do?*' (6; cp. 22:10). Jesus said that he was to go to Damascus where he would be told what he must do. Saul was to write some years afterwards, '*We make it our aim ... to be well pleasing to him*' (2 Corinthians 5:9). **An evidence of conversion to Christ is submission to his lordship in our lives.** Those who love the Lord Jesus will keep his commandments (John 14:15). Have you submitted to the lordship of Christ in your life?

The persecutor of the church was transformed the day he met the Lord Jesus. His hatred of the Saviour was replaced by great love and devotion to him. He became the apostle Paul, and he was the greatest Christian missionary. He planted churches throughout what is now known as Turkey, and also in Macedonia and Greece. The New Testament contains some of his letters to churches, friends and Christian workers.

Everyone will meet the Lord Jesus

We do not know when the Lord Jesus will come again. His second coming will be wonderful for the Christian, but it will be terrible for those who die in unbelief. Their bodies will also be raised and they will meet God to face divine judgement (Matthew 25:31-46; John 5:28-29; 2 Thessalonians 1:7-9). We can be prepared, if we repent of our sin, trust in him, and follow him. We will then know that our sins are forgiven and we will enjoy peace with God.

The Lord Jesus gives further teaching on his power to raise the dead and about his authority to judge the world (cp. 21-22). He speaks in these verses of two resurrections — the bringing of dead sinners to spiritual life, and the resurrection of all mankind at his second coming.

When we are born again, we are brought out of a state of spiritual death into life (24; cp. Ephesians 2:1,5). God freely forgives us our sins and we no longer fear judgement. Spiritual life comes through hearing the voice of the Son of God through his word. Jesus said, '*The hour is coming, and now is, when the dead will hear the voice of the Son of God; and those who hear will live*' (25; cp. Romans 10:17).

The Lord Jesus speaks of his second coming when all the dead will be raised. '*All who are in the graves will hear his voice and come forth — those who have done good, to the resurrection of life, and those who have done evil, to the resurrection of condemnation*' (28-29). Everyone who has ever lived will hear his voice, even though they have returned to dust! That voice brings forth life and this is a great miracle (Lazarus, four days dead, heard Christ's voice and was raised, 11:43-44). We shall see our blessed Saviour and we shall have new resurrection bodies that will never know pain, illness or death (Philippians 3:20-21; 1 John 3:2-3). **Will the return of the Lord Jesus be a day of terror or of rejoicing for you? Are you ready to meet him?**

If you want to know more about the Christian faith or would like to continue to read the Bible, please speak to the person who gave you this booklet. They may also be able to provide you with regular Bible reading notes for each day of the year.

Other titles by Alec Taylor

French, German and Slovak language editions of this booklet have also been published.

A Pilgrim's Treasury — 366 daily devotional readings from each book of the Bible (published by EP Books) and **available through your Christian bookshop (not from Alec Taylor).**

The Promise — 31 daily Bible readings introducing the Christian message (published by the Banner of Truth Trust) and **available through your Christian bookshop (not from Alec Taylor).**
The Promise has also been published in French, Spanish, German and Slovak.

Pilgrim Bible Notes — published each month and covering complete books of the Bible. The Scriptures are simply explained in these devotional notes. These can be downloaded from the 'God's Glory our Joy' website: www.ggoj.org.uk

The Holy Trinity — a Bible study leaflet which supplies ample Bible references to show that the Lord Jesus Christ is God, that the Holy Spirit, a Person, is God. The teaching of the Holy Trinity is then proved from Scripture.